The Chore Solution: Making Families Better by Working Together

The Chore Solution: Making Families Better by Working Together

Jason J. and Ann Cowan

Illustrations by Bryan T. Jones

Library of Congress Control Number: 2010911666
ISBN: Hardcover   978-1-4535-5448-7
                Softcover   978-1-4535-5447-0
                Ebook   978-1-4535-5449-4

This book was printed in the United States of America.

To order additional copies of this book, contact:
Xlibris Corporation
1-888-795-4274
www.Xlibris.com
Orders@Xlibris.com
84389

Contents

For our little angels
or, depending on the day,
our little delightful challenges:

Bryan Jones
Andrew Jones
Gavin Cowan
Ares Cowan

Acknowledgments

We would like to thank the following people without whose help this book, as it is written, would not have been possible:

Rosanne and Terry Cowan for their help in reviewing, editing, and encouraging us to write it in the first place, thank you.

Audrey and Jim Thompson for the support and the many calls throughout the development of the Web site, thank you.

Jamie Lucas for his help in editing and the many marketing ideas for this system, thank you.

Don Evans and Curt MacInnis for their input and ideas, thank you.

Jenna Bertapelle for taking the photos on such short notice, thank you.

Finally, to our supporters on Facebook, your encouragement means a lot to us, thank you.

Foreword

We were so sick and tired of always feeling like bad parents. The house is a mess; there is a shortage of clean clothes, and there is no time or possible way to catch up. There is always a new video game or DVD or the latest toy or trend that everyone else has, and if they don't, they will feel like outsiders. We felt that there had to be a way to balance between spending too much money and trying to make sure the kids had the things they want in order to have a happier household for everyone.

We have talked to several parents, and they all had the same complaints. "Every time we go to the store, our kids ask for something, we *have* to get it, or else they . . ." Ann has even had strangers offer to buy the children candy because of the scene our wonderful brood was causing. Ah, the joys of being a parent.

The question that we had, How can we get them all to be motivated to do chores and do it fairly so the work is spread evenly? The answer is, *we* don't—*they* do.

In this book, we are going to look at the challenges of balancing money and sanity. We will also tell you how we overcame these challenges and offer suggestions for how you can do the same.

Challenge 1: Everyone can afford it.

We have tried to give an allowance, and we have tried to pay as we go. This only hurt our pocketbook. It seems that we lost control over our spending, and we lost track of how much we were dishing out. When we reviewed our budget, we were surprised and appalled to learn how much extra we were spending.

Challenge 2: Less stress. The idea of waking up to a messy house and trying to start each day in the middle of chaos is overwhelming. We have so many projects that are half started, never to be finished because the dishes need to be cleaned or the trash taken out. These are simple tasks that are time-consuming enough to take you offtrack. The house will never be cleaned because we are always distracted. Imagine waking up to a swept hallway or dusted windowsills. Little things add up to nirvana.

Challenge 3: Chores to be set by age and ability. Our ten-year-old wanted to mow the lawn. "Riding the lawn mower is so much fun!" he says. We agreed. After about an hour and a half, we looked out into the backyard and saw our own personal English garden maze. It took us twice as long to get the lawn mowed that weekend. This made us realize that having a ten-year-old mow the lawn maybe was not such a good idea.

Challenge 4: Experts and paying for chores. Some experts may disagree about paying children for chores—we are not experts, nor do we claim to be experts. We are merely parents; therefore, we can do whatever we want to "ruin" our own children. (Of course, we are writing this in a tongue-in-cheek spirit.) We are parents, and we want the best for our children. It is an amazing feeling to watch our selfish little monster turn into a beautiful ray of sunshine because he did something for himself.

Challenge 5: When is the proper age to start? "My child is too young to understand that she benefits from being paid for doing her chores, or my child has already been conditioned that he doesn't have to help around the house." These are common reactions from parents that we have spoken with. We believe that at every age, children can help. We have four children ranging from a teenager to a five-month-old. Upon starting this, it felt as if they were all asking for too much too often. We were getting overwhelmed with all the requests.

The five-month-old is a little too young to do chores, little to no motor skills are hampering him. But to watch him watch his older brothers, he can't wait until he gets on the payroll. We do pay him for smiles and giggles but deduct for dirty diapers and crying. So far, he has come out even.

Challenge 6: Dream and dream big. Children have different views about what is essential for living than adults. Unfortunately, many of us adults have outgrown the dream of receiving a pony for our birthday. Children deserve to have these dreams and goals. They deserve to live in a wonderland. They also deserve to be given a chance to earn and work for their dreams.

Challenge 7 "I spent all my money. Can I have $20 for . . . ?" We got through the first month of the chore system, and as expected, one of the children had burned through everything he earned in a week. We had things showing up at the house that were ordered with the newfound money. Then we were asked shortly after for some additional money because he was going to a county fair with his girlfriend.

These are the types of challenges that we have encountered. You may encounter more or less. You may have different challenges. This book is designed to walk you through the chore system we created and tailor it to your specific needs.

So let's get started! There are some questions in here that require you to realize what you are already paying for, the dreams that you and your children have, and what is appropriate for your situation.

 *(As you read, we suggest you get a pen and use the note pages starting on page 41 for your personal reflections.)*

You will be designing your own chore system to fit the needs of your family. We will show you how we resolved these challenges and how you can adapt this idea to fit your lifestyle.

Challenge 1: Everyone can afford it

Times are hard, we know. When we started this, we were afraid that we wouldn't have the extra money to pay for all these chores that were set up. I was more afraid that we would make a promise to the most important people in our life and not be able to follow through. We were barely making our bills. We were arguing about how to make it fair for everyone and still have enough money to do things that we wanted—the fun stuff. Our family is a blended family with the children ranging from ages of months into midteens. What is fun for our fifteen-year-old was too advanced for our six-year-old. What our ten-year-old was into was different from any of the others.

Stop. Think about this. In a month, how many movies do you rent for your kids, how many trips to the store to buy their favorite snacks, or how many times do you buy the new and best video game, *ever?*

(Get your pen and paper out—write down everything, and we mean everything, that you have gotten extra for your family this month. Page 42)

This is where the chore money comes from. One month for one child, we spent more than $300 on extra stuff that he had to have and we couldn't afford. The average chore amount that he receives every month is around $50. He sticks to that budget. Needless to say, we don't begrudge the children extras. We just enjoy giving them these extras more than ever. It is so nice to hear, "Thanks! But I could've gotten that myself." Spending an extra $20 here and there, added to the $50, chore money is nice compared to the $300 previously spent.

We consider extras to be anything that we don't want to or have to buy. Here are some examples that we consider to be extras with an approximate dollar amount for each purchase:

Video game	$60
Fast food	$2
Trip to the movies	$10
Movie and game rentals	$15
Hot wheel cars	$15
Random gotta-have toys	$10

Remember when we were kids. The things that we had to play with were usually outside or came in a box and had a folding piece of cardboard that we moved pieces around. They were called board games. Pac-Man and Space Invaders were hot games, and you had to leave your house to play them. Our parents had it worse off yet. They had to walk to school, in the snow, uphill both ways! (I don't even think that they had toys.) There are so many choices for kids to do today. Most of these choices are expensive, compared to a whiffed ball and bat. Now there are three different home game systems with a myriad of the latest and greatest games that are released every month. There are several portable game systems with games for them. Of course you have to buy a couple copies of each so they can play with each other on their own portable game system. There are MP3 players from many electronics companies. There are cell phones, a ton of building-block toy sets, skateboards, and accessories for all these. It's a lot different from when we were happy with a bike, a ball, and a kite.

Furthermore, each kid has many friends. Each of those friends has different combinations of all these things. However, when the kids come home, they tell you all about how Nate has this or Griffin has that, and it sounds like every kid out there has everything money can buy. It's a little intimidating when you look at everything they just have to have.

Because of the new must-have expenses, this system has taught the boys that they may have to prioritize what they want. They may have to make a list of the things they want and budget and save for an extra special item. In addition, they have learned to be less influenced by peer pressure because they have to distinguish between what everyone else has and what they really want. Our fifteen-year-old would like a classic car; he won't be able to make that amount of money in a month, but over time, his chore money will help supplement his part-time job income.

We used to go to the store as if we were covert spies, lying to the kids, telling them we had something to do. They would ask if we were going to the store. In unison, we would reply no. Taking the children to the store with us, let's say, was not something we looked forward to. It was stressful to have to say "no, put that back" over and over and over again. The poor dears would be frustrated and say one of my all-time favorite kid's lines, "You *never* get me *anything*." (I remember saying this to my parents.) Eyes are rolling on both sides of the grocery cart. "*Fine*!" we say through our teeth. Not to receive a reply of, "*Thanks*, guys, you're the greatest." No, usually the reply was a sideways grin of satisfaction—that they tricked their parents again. They are smarter than us, and they know it. Then we get home from the store. We grab our usual ten bags and the milk. We meet at the door. They are holding their new treasure and waiting for us to open it. On top of this, the little cherubs were leaving little messes all over the place. The six-year-old was leaving straw wrappers out for us to throw away, the ten-year-old would spill cereal all over the floor for us to sweep up, and the fifteen-year-old would leave his granola bar wrappers on the floor *in front* of the garbage can. It was so overwhelming. We are not saying that we are perfect either; even we would leave things out or make little messes. We needed to work on our self-discipline as well.

Now they know that they get a little extra for helping carry in the groceries. They don't get any extra for opening the door for us, which they do. They now understand that with ten bags of groceries and the milk, it is nearly impossible to open a door. Also, since they get charged for leaving messes and not cleaning them up, they have been much better about cleaning up after themselves. They are actually reminding us when we leave things out that we need to be responsible and pick our messes up as well.

The money is there; we are already spending it on the children. You can adjust the pay scale based on your situation.

The chores that we have assigned also have time lines to ensure that we won't be taken advantage of, not that our little angels would ever think to do such a thing. Sweeping and mopping are paid weekly. Even if they sweep and mop every day, they only get paid for it one time a week. The rules are clear. We had a family meeting and went over each chore and the amount of money attached. We gave the boys two days to decide if the chores were fair and to suggest changes. Because they had input, they felt empowered from the first day. And we felt relief. The relief that we feel comes from knowing there shouldn't be future requests for more money here and there. The boys all agreed that this was a great system. We do have to remind them that this is the money they have until the next time they are paid. If they run out in the middle of the month, it isn't our fault. This has taught the children how to utilize their spending to budget for what they need and want.

Look back at your list and see all the small things that your child could have bought for himself. See all the things that, at the time, were important for them to have and all the extra money you spent. Do you think that they would be so free with their own money? If they are, let them; it is their money.

Challenge 2: Less stress

Stress will not magically disappear simply because your kids are now empowered to go shopping for themselves. Based on personal experience, you may simply have less stress for everyday chores. They will still need to be reminded, and they will still not feel like doing them. The wonderful thing is that if they don't do the chores, they don't get paid. You do.

Yes, that's right. When we see that their chore isn't complete, we will do it and announce that we just made X amount of money. When updating your chore board (the chore board and how to set it up is described later in the book in the "Solution" chapter), update the amount that you earned—making a point to let them know that this was money that they missed out on. Soon, chores will be done proudly and before you can get to them. That is the goal.

When everyday chores are complete, everyone will have more time to do what they enjoy. You could even pop real popcorn and sit in front of the TV, all together in a clean living room, finding the remote with ease because it isn't buried in the cluttered couch. Maybe you just want to go to the park with the children and watch them play after having a picnic. You might want to just go for a walk or a bike ride. All the ideas listed above have little to do with spending money. This is a lesson we learned when we were kids: you can still have fun without spending money. Whatever your nirvana is, you can find it.

Remember, your kids are your kids. You will know what motivates them the most. If you don't, ask them, give them time to think of an answer, and then jump all over it.

 *(It's time to write again. Make a list of all your stresses. If possible, have your kids do the same. This is a private exercise you can decide to share with each other or not. Page 43)*

Let's not be selfish; less stress isn't only for you. Without you complaining and grumbling, your kids will feel less stressed as well. Even when they don't master their chore to your expectations, be proud that they are doing their chore. Tell them thank you. Give them a hug. Let them know that they are helping out the family and you appreciate it.

It was a rare cool summer day, and we opened the windows of the house. We had to run out for probably another gallon of milk, thanks to the chocolate milk monsters that we have living with us. We were out at the store, and it started raining. *Raining* isn't a strong-enough word. A torrential downpour commenced. We left the boys at home. Usually, this would have meant nothing. We just hurried up, got our milk, and rushed home to shut the windows and mop up the rain that we knew had accumulated under them. To our utmost surprise, our ten-year-old took care of shutting all the windows. Because of his initiative, he got an extra bonus for the chores that month. He wasn't expecting to get paid for this task, but he did it anyway. We chose to give a bonus in this case because we felt that it was warranted. Of course, bonuses aren't given all the time.

Look over your private list. Now imagine all the stresses that you have. Imagine they would be eased by living in a pleasant place full of love and helpful, grateful people. We make sure to reward them with praise when they go the extra mile. Furthermore, we remind them that when everyone works together, a lot more gets done and we can be in a much cleaner and more enjoyable place. They have more confidence because they are proud of their accomplishments and because they are helping the family. They are a lot happier because they don't have to hear harping and nagging to do chores. As a result, we are a lot happier because things are getting done without having to constantly pester them.

Challenge 3: Chores to be set by age and ability

One challenge we had was to set the chore list to be fair to every child. There are many Web sites that suggest what age and what chore. We just sat down one evening and brainstormed to fit our needs. Either way, make sure that your child can handle the chore you set for them.

Here is a chore list suggestion by age that we found using random Internet searches:

2-3 years old (The Helpers)

1. Help put laundry away
2. Help pick up their messes
3. Help feed pets.

4-5 years old (The Advanced Helpers)

1. Help put away groceries
2. Help prepare meals
3. Dust

6-8 years old (The Not-A-Baby Helpers)

1. Vacuum and mop
2. Take care of pets
3. Take out trash

9-12 years old (The Beginning of Independence)

1. Help wash the cars
2. Wash dishes
3. Clean the bathrooms

13+ years old (Hectic Schedulers)

1. All of the laundry
2. Clean refrigerators
3. Wash Windows

 *(Writing time. Think about what your children would like to do to help you. Page 44)*

Do not listen to advice. We have heard from people things like "*My* little seven-year-old hand washes the dishes to perfection." What is wrong with this kid? Do not try to compare your kids with other kids. Some parents may lie for one reason or another. Or a softer way to say it, they may stretch the truth. Remember, you know your kids best.

When your kids want to try a new advanced chore, let them, safely under your supervision. We let them try the chore for no compensation so they can see if they can do it and be added to that chore.

We have had to rearrange chores to fit each child.

Challenge 4: Experts and paying for chores

Clearly, there are arguments both ways about paying children for chores. One argument is that children need to learn a sense of duty to family and will, thusly, do chores out of the goodness of their wonderful little hearts.

We love this idea. The reality is that some children need to be reminded to do their chores to the point of driving parents crazy, and it becomes more of a punishment than a sense of duty.

Recently, we saw an interview with Warren Buffett. We can all agree that Warren Buffett is a successful man. However, in this interview, we learned something about Warren Buffett that tells us he is successful not because of money, but because he has a true understanding of what's important in life. What he shared was the best gift he ever had from his father: unconditional love. He clarified that it was unconditional, not uncriticized love. (Bay 2010) From this brief statement, I believe he meant that no matter what, children should be absolutely loved by us, and that love is not used as a tool to get what we want. However, we still retain the right to constructively criticize and help them grow into better people.

What are we getting at here? Basically, what we are saying is that we learn a sense of loyalty to our family from unconditional love. Being paid or not being paid for chores seems petty and inconsequential.

Another argument against paying children for chores is that by doing this, we teach them to be all about money rather than doing things for the good of others. We fully understand this point of view.

 *(What do you think about paying your children for chores? Should they be paid for everything or just certain chores? Page 45)*

From our personal experience with paying for chores, we observed that our children were proud to have earned what they bought. They were equally proud to go to the bank and start their own bank accounts to save what they had earned. Additionally, our fifteen-year-old son felt more like an adult because he had gotten his own debit card from the bank. (Even though the card has his name stamped on it, the card is in our name because he's under eighteen.) Also, we were finding that the children were asking for things and getting things anyway, but chores weren't getting done. We were getting frustrated, and the boys were learning that they could just ask for whatever they want and they didn't have to do anything for it. What's the point of that statement? People want things and it's okay, provided we understand that they are only material possessions and we don't put the acquisition of those possessions above the well-being of others. We believe teaching children to *earn* what they want is a valuable lesson. They have a greater appreciation for what they get, and they are empowered to get what they want if they choose to achieve their goals. Even when they want to buy their items, they will sometimes want to go to places like the Salvation Army or Goodwill to save money. We take this a step further and explain to them that by shopping at these stores, they are actually helping others. We have explained that these stores take donations and rehab them for sale. The money earned on the items goes to charity.

Once we move out on our own, we have to earn everything by working for it for the rest of our lives. Why would we teach something different to our children as they are growing up? Wouldn't this leave them ill prepared to survive on their own? Our goal as parents is to raise competent adults that can not only survive but also thrive as they go out into the real world.

Finally, our children have a sense of family because they are truly part of our family and not just little people that are around. No matter how many chores they do or how many messes they make, we give unconditional love because they are our family.

We are not trying to say that some experts are wrong. As was stated in the beginning of the book, we are not experts. I am merely pointing out that the observations that we have made from our experiences using this method suggest a different conclusion. As always, we encourage everyone to make their own observations and formulate their own beliefs.

Challenge 5: When is the proper age to start?

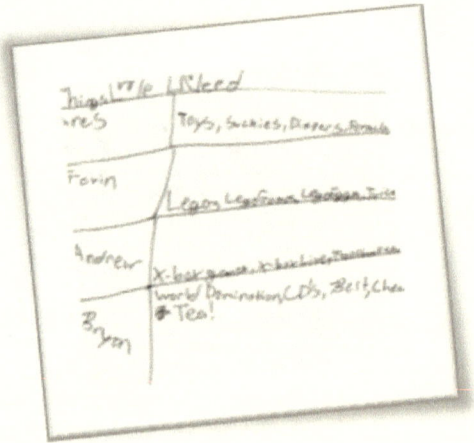

We have four children living at home. Let me introduce them to you. Bryan is fifteen. Andrew is ten. Gavin is six. Ares is five months. We have a wide range of ages and demands. And we love them all.

Bryan is very artistic. He likes great music, and we encourage him to be himself. He is Ann's first son, and the first grandson in the family. He has a strong feeling of entitlement. Did I mention that he is a teenager? His biggest challenge with this system is the pay, of course. He has been known to add various chore descriptions to see if he can get extra money.

Unfortunately, for him, the side of the house still counts as part of the yard when he mows the lawn. No extra money for doing a complete job. He understands this yet continues to write various "work order" slips, hoping that we give in. (Work order slips are our way of tracking what chores are performed and are explained in the "Solution" chapter.) The solution to this is we don't give in, and it is just extra work for him to fill in more slips.

Andrew is our comic. He tells us jokes that are funny to every other ten-year-old. Ann encourages this, much to Jason's chagrin. Andrew is also into sports and can guess the most outrageous outcomes, which usually come true. Andrew is the second child. He was Ann's youngest child for nine years, and now he's the middle child. The biggest challenge that we have with Andrew and chores is focus. If the television is on, you can forget even trying to get him to do anything. He'll start, and about ten seconds into it, he will be distracted. The solution to this is to remind him that his chore should take a specified amount of time, and so we set a timer.

Gavin is the problem solver. He is a very clever boy. He is Jason's first son. He was an only child, and now he is the middle of four boys. His ability to adapt to any situation and find a solution to any given problem is remarkable. The biggest challenge with him is finding chores that will give him the opportunity to use his imagination, so he will enjoy doing them. The solution to this was to make games out of the chores. One of his favorites is to take care of empty boxes. He stands at the top of the basement stairs and hurls them down. Then he goes down and hurls all the boxes into the designated corner of the basement.

Having a new baby makes chores a bigger deal for us. We can't do it all by ourselves. Having the kids help out gives us a chance to breathe.

(It's that time again. Get out your paper and write down a description of your kids. What do you think their challenges will be and what will be your solutions? Page 46)

We believe the proper time to start organizing a chore plan is right now. It doesn't matter how old or young your kids are. They can do things to help.

This is a self-motivated form of achieving goals that begins with constant reminders. The reminders aren't as constant anymore. The boys now say, "I know, I know. If I want something, I have to earn it." They quickly calculate how much the item is and how long it will take them at their current rate of pay. Sometimes they are satisfied to wait. Other times they step up to the challenge and find chores not listed to do. They don't have to ask to do extras. They understand that we have the final say in approving the chore and paying. On the other hand, they realize that the "unauthorized" chore they do may not be paid. Either way, we always make sure to say thank you for their help. They simply cannot get what they want without doing their chores.

Challenge 6: Dream and dream big

We believe that you should encourage your children to dream first and do second. If we didn't have goals, this book would never have been written. What are your goals, all your goals no matter how silly you, or others, may think they are?

(Write down all your goals. Be outrageous. No one else has to see them. This is just for you. If possible, have your kids do this too. Page 47)

Why can't your children have the same outrageous goals? My fifteen-year-old wants a classic Corvette, the ten-year-old wants to be a professional football player, and the six-year-old wants the largest Lego collection in the whole world. If we told them that they will never achieve these things, then we are stomping on their dreams. They could still achieve this, but it would be harder without our support. We also know that goals and dreams change as one gets older. Why crush their dreams?

This isn't a challenge in our family, but we have heard the excuse that "my *teenager* isn't motivated by money." Are you kidding me? Everyone has goals and dreams. If your kids are different, isn't it time to instill dreaming and reaching for certain goals? This scenario scares me. If a teenager isn't motivated to have the freedom of getting what they want, how are they going to be useful in society as an adult?

We have lists of what each one of us wants. We have dream walls. We took pictures or downloaded pictures of what we all want. Some are easily achievable and some will take harder work and a longer time to achieve, but all are achievable! All are achievable? *Yes.* We switch out the picture when they achieve what they want or when their dreams change. We put no limits on the price or the amount of goals they have. The dream wall is in constant motion.

This is another important point about the dream wall. Our dreams are constantly changing. As the fifteen-year-old matures, he might decide that he wants a different car, or he may get the car that he wants. As the ten-year-old learns to play football and be a team player, he may decide that he wants to teach others rather than become a player himself. As the six-year-old grows, he may decide that he wants to design and build buildings rather than just playing with building blocks. As we grow, our dreams evolve.

When we set goals, we decide where we are going. In our experience throughout life, whenever we set a goal, a *true* goal, then the path toward that goal eventually formulates in some fashion. For example, we have a lot of things we would like to do, such as build a car and take a trip across the country on old Route 66 in that car. When people saw or heard about our chore system, they were excited to start it for their children. We decided we could help more people by writing this book. This book is potentially a path toward that goal. The idea for this book came from a desire to reach that goal. If we don't get there from publishing this book, then we will find another way.

The bottom line is that we are teaching our children that when they have goals, they need to work toward making those goals happen. The fifteen-year-old has been given the opportunity to illustrate this book and be paid for it. This is teaching him that sometimes, when you have a strong-enough goal and the opportunities arise to reach that goal, you need to grab onto them and make it happen. Eventually, the younger ones will be taught this lesson, but first, they need to learn how to work toward their respective goals. Without the discipline instilled from doing chores to reach their goals, we cannot guide them to the next step—to learn how to discover their own paths. Also, we emphasize that by helping others, you may benefit from your efforts.

We believe that by promoting goal setting and goal achievement, we are teaching them to not only survive but also exceed their expectations in life. Money is merely a tool to achieve goals. In the same respect, the chore list is a tool to help them achieve their goals.

Challenge 7: "I spent all my money. Can I have $20 for . . . ?"

Following the first month, and probably many more, of paying the children for chores, you may hear "I spent all my money and I need $20 for (*fill in the blank*)." There is a very important point to be made here regarding the lesson about money management. When the request for money comes, and it will, the answer must be undeniably no. The problem is that if we give in to the request for money, the lesson that when the money is gone, *it's gone* will not be learned. We ran into this challenge and realized that if we gave in and handed out just $20 for whatever, it would be as if we were teaching the lesson that it doesn't matter if you spend all your money because we'll always be there to give more.

Instead, we held fast and refused. We believe that we need to teach all of them that when you work for money, it has value to you because of the effort you put in for it. If we send them out into the real world with the belief that parents will always bail them out when they need a little extra, then we are teaching them that they can spend all their salary in the first week and forget about things like rent and utility bills and phone bills.

 *(Get out that pencil; try to think of all the extras the kids may hit you up for. Write down creative ways of saying no. Page 48)*

We cannot stress this point enough. The kids know how to pull at your heartstrings, but it is very important to resist the urge to give up the extra money. We would much rather have our children realize this lesson when the mistake is only a $20 or $30 mistake. They need to be more responsible with their money before they are out in the real world, and it becomes a $500 or $1,000 mistake—or worse.

Let's remember that a part of the goal is to teach financial responsibility. We're not saying, by any means, that we are trying to teach that nobody can afford anything. We believe that we should always try to have a mind-set that we can afford anything we want, but we choose not to buy it because we have different priorities at certain times. Life is all about choices, and this is the message we are trying to relay.

Our goal is to help them learn to live fruitful, happy lives rather than constantly be stressed out about the bills that can't be paid because they spent everything on games and fast food. Both of us have been in that situation before, and know how hard it is to get out. By teaching the kids now about budgeting, we are hoping that they understand how to spend their money wisely. And that this will help later when they are on their own. We know this sounds harsh, but the reality is that the world can be harsh. Wouldn't it be better for our children if they go out on their own with the understanding that they can have everything they want, over time? The alternative would be the lesson that the real world doesn't care if you are out of money because it's not their concern. The landlord doesn't care if you can't pay; he just wants his money. The utility company doesn't care; they want their money. The grocery store doesn't care; they want their money. Wouldn't it be better for our children to be able to get the house and car and lifestyle that they want than to have multiple creditors making phone calls and harassing them about when they're going to pay their payments?

The reality is that lessons about money are much easier to learn when you can't pay for a movie on Friday night with your girlfriend than when you can't pay for your car note. So we've stressed this point enough. We try to make sure that we don't just give in because it's easier to give an extra $10 or $20 than to deal with complaining. We are helping much more by doing the right thing here, so our suggestion is to stand firm in saying no, or the whole chore system becomes ineffective.

The Solution: The Chore System.

So we have covered many challenges. You still may have your own surprising challenges that spring up. *Do not worry.* Just amend the system to fit your needs.

We have included a picture of our chore space on page. This is a list of system stuff that we use.

1.   Chalkboard, whiteboard, or poster board.
2.   Some sort of container large enough to hold chore slips for one month.
3.   A reminder of what their responsibilities are.
4.   Chore slips available with a pencil.

The chore system consists of many simple elements. When all these elements are used together, it is the ultimate system to keep track of chores, to inspire the kids to do chores, and to make it easier for us as parents.

The first element that I want to explain is the chore chart, page. This is a screenshot of our chore list. We have it in a frame in the chore corner of our dining room. We selected various chores and then assigned the length of time to complete the chore or how often they can do the chore. Of these chores, we then chose who was responsible to do them and how much each chore was worth. For example, the living room needed to be swept and mopped each week. We felt that Andrew (age ten) would be the best for this chore.

We have a method to track the chores, which is to have the boys fill out work orders (see page 38) to let us know what they have done. It is clear to the boys that we have ultimate control over what is or isn't an acceptable completion of a task. These work orders are then placed in a box so they won't get lost. An additional benefit, especially for the younger boys, is that they are constantly getting better at their penmanship from filling out the work orders.

At some frequency, be it every week or every other week, we tally these work orders and track the progress of each of the boys. We have developed a spreadsheet to track the pay for each individual, including ourselves. We will explain here how to set it up by yourself when you want to do that.

In the first column, we list the description of each chore. There is one chore per row. The second column lists the duration or the length of time allowed for completion of this chore. The reasoning behind this is because we didn't want the lawn being mowed every day so the eldest could earn $70 per week. Another example is that we gave a higher-paying job that was somewhat easier for the six-year-old so the chore is paid monthly. The third column lists who performs each chore. This is necessary due to the difference in the ages of our kids. Some of the chores can be done by any of them and are listed as "all." The fourth column lists the dollar amount paid for each chore. Finally, the last columns before we get to the calculations are one column for each child's name and one for us, which lists the number of times each chore is done for that month.

The calculations are in the next several columns. Again, we have a column for each boy and one for ourselves. The formula in each of those columns resembles this: =F3*$D3. We take the dollar amount column and multiply it by the "number of times the chore was performed" column to give us a dollar amount under each boy's name. At the bottom of these columns, the formula resembles this: =SUM(J3:J20). This simply sums up the dollar amounts for each individual.

This tab in the file represents one month's worth of chores. This same sheet can then be copied eleven more times, and each tab can be named with months of the year. By setting the spreadsheet up this way, it becomes relatively simple and automatic to track what everyone has earned. You simply take the work orders and tally them in the columns, telling you how many times each child has done each chore. In figure 3 (on page 39), you can see the tally columns that show, for instance, that Bryan has mowed the front lawn and mowed the back lawn twice in the month. In the sum column for Bryan, this shows automatically as $10 for each chore. At the bottom of Bryan's column, it sums up those two chores along with every other chore that he did that month to give us the complete dollar amount that he should get paid for the month. This number, as we update it, is recorded on the whiteboard for each child so they can see their progress for the month.

It is important for children to see the amounts they earn each week even though they don't get paid until the end of the month. By seeing their progress during the month and having a dollar amount shown for each goal they have to achieve, they know how close they are and how much more they need to do. Achievement of their goals is completely up to them and tracked and displayed throughout the month on a weekly or biweekly basis.

The amount of time you spend doing this is minimal. We update the chore board every two weeks. Sometimes more often if we see that we are doing all the work. To update the chore spreadsheet, simply take the work orders and record the number of times each chore was done by each child. Extras are recorded in the dollar columns at whatever rate we determine. For all chores entered, including extras, you will need to do the math to add to what's already been done and enter the correct number.

When the sums of the dollar amounts are posted on the whiteboard quite frequently, our total is higher than what theirs is. The boys do not like having their parents on the board with more money than they have. This encourages them to work even harder. One final point to notice from the chore list is that we deduct for messes and things left out. That's right, we take $0.50 away from their total for every time they leave a straw wrapper or don't put away the game controller or leave a plate out. This has paid infinite dividends toward keeping things clean in the house. We also do this for bad habits that we want to change, like leaning on the back of the couch or spinning in chairs. Use this method to try to eliminate whatever pet peeve you may have. At the same time, we have also made it available to the children to remind us to put things away that we've left out or done wrong. In this way, we can use this to get reminders of things we need to change as well.

 *(*Look over your notes to see how simple this chore system will be for you to implement into your household! This is the time for you to add or subtract your ideas to make this chore system work for you and your family. And this is the last time you have to write anything, we promise! *Page 49)*

Conclusion

Abracadabra! No need to wave that magic wand of yours, no need to sprinkle your magic dust—all your problems have been solved!

Well, maybe not. As we said before, we are not claiming to be experts. We have just created this system, and it has worked well for us. Everyone that we have told about it absolutely loves it. We wanted to spread the news to more people. In a crazy world, we found some relief from stress and have been able to get more done with less hassle. We wanted to offer this solution to others in the hopes that it might help more people get the same results. Also, we feel it's a helpful tool to assist in teaching responsibility and work ethic.

Personally, we have noticed many benefits. The boys have learned to work in teams to get their chores done—faster. Since we don't tell them when to do chores, they have to manage their time between homework, friends, and chores. After they complete a chore, they are very proud of the work they have done. When they see something that needs to be done, usually they just do it with little to no prodding. They feel empowered to spend their own money, which they earned. Their sense of ownership has grown, and they are proud of their purchases. As a result, they take better care of their purchased items.

Bryan surfaced from his room and sought out his younger brother. We, of course, thought that Andrew once again violated Bryan's personal space. You see, the boys would sneak around and borrow each other's things. We were expecting to hear the shouting match that usually follows such a crime. Instead, Bryan *actually* asked Andrew if he could play one of Andrew's video games. Andrew said, "Sure, whatever." But as parents, we heard, "Yes, my dear brother. I love you and thank you for asking first." Another surprising but wonderful benefit is that they are showing more respect for each other's things.

In addition, they are learning to set goals and be more responsible with money. We have empowered them to have some control over their attainment of goals. They are learning to be more responsible with money because they are learning that what they want takes work to earn. Also, they are learning that everything is about choices. When they have $20 to spend and they want three different things that cost $20, they have to choose what is most important to them. Further, they are learning to be more frugal with money by buying things that are on sale or from discounted stores such as the Salvation Army and Goodwill. With this, we teach them that they are supporting charities by saving money if they buy at Salvation Army or Goodwill.

The result for us has been reduced stress, teaching valuable life lessons to our children and saving money and time. We don't claim to be experts on this or even claim that this is right for everyone. However, we are saying that this may help you and that everyone should make their own choices as to how they might use this tool to better their life.

Best wishes,

J and Ann

Chores

Chore	Duration	Who's Responsible	Amount
Mow Front Lawn	Weekly	Bryan	$5.00
Mow Back Lawn	Weekly	Bryan	$5.00
Sweep and mop Livinig Room	Weekly	Andrew	$2.00
Sweep and mop Kitchen and Nook	Weekly	Andrew	$2.00
Load Dishwasher	Daily	All	$0.25
Unload Dishwasher	Daily	All	$0.25
Take boxes downstairs	Monthly	Gavin	$5.00
Dust	Weekly	Gavin	$1.00
Take trash out	Weekly	Andrew & Bryan	$1.00
Bring cans in	Weekly	Andrew & Bryan	$1.00
Fill juice in refrigerator	As req'd	Gavin	$1.00
Babysitting	Hourly	All	$5.00
Laundry (Hangers, put away)	Weekly	All	$1.00
Clean Bedrooms	Weekly	All	$2.00
Make Dinner	Daily	All	$0.50
*Extras			
Leaving anything out (toys, movies, games, etc.)	Each Occurance	All	($0.50)
Leaving trash out	Each Occurance	All	($0.50)

*Extras include extra work. For example, if you help clean the garage, wash cars, pick up the yard, clean the bathrooms, etc., you will get extra money.
Everything will be checked upon completion. Jason and Ann have the right to refuse payment if the work is not done well. We also expect not to have to remind you to do things. If we do them you will not get paid.
We all need to work together, if you help someone you will not be paid for their chore, but they may help you in return.

Please fill out the chore slip and put it into the box for credit.

Figure 1: Chore Chart

Chores

_____
Name

_____
Chore

_____
Date

Entered by:
_____

Figure 2: Work Order

Chores

Chore	Duration	Who's Respons	Amount	Bryan	Andrew	Gavin	Jason & Ann	Bryan	Andrew	Gavin	Jason & Ann
Mow Front Lawn	Weekly	Bryan	$5.00	2				$10.00	$0.00	$0.00	$0.00
Mow Back Lawn	Weekly	Bryan	$5.00	2				$10.00	$0.00	$0.00	$0.00
Sweep and mop Living Room	Weekly	Andrew	$2.00		1		1	$0.00	$2.00	$0.00	$2.00
Sweep and mop Kitchen and Nook	Weekly	Andrew	$2.00		1		1	$0.00	$2.00	$0.00	$2.00
Load Dishwasher	Daily	All	$0.25	1	1	2	29	$0.25	$0.25	$0.50	$7.25
Unload Dishwasher	Daily	All	$0.25	1	3		29	$0.25	$0.75	$0.00	$7.25
Take boxes downstairs	Monthly	Gavin	$5.00			1		$0.00	$0.00	$5.00	$0.00
Dust	Weekly	Gavin	$1.00					$0.00	$0.00	$0.00	$0.00
Take trash out	Weekly	Andrew & Bryan	$1.00	1	1		2	$1.00	$1.00	$0.00	$2.00
Bring cans in	Weekly	Andrew & Bryan	$1.00	1	1		1	$1.00	$1.00	$0.00	$1.00
Fill juice in refrigerator	As req'd	Gavin	$1.00			2		$0.00	$0.00	$2.00	$0.00
Babysitting	Hourly	All	$5.00	3	3	0.4		$15.00	$15.00	$2.00	$0.00
Laundry (Hangers, put away)	Weekly	All	$1.00	1	2	2	2	$1.00	$2.00	$2.00	$2.00
Clean Bedrooms	Weekly	All	$2.00	2	2	2		$4.00	$4.00	$4.00	$0.00
Make Dinner	Daily	All	$0.50		1	1	29	$0.00	$0.50	$0.50	$14.50
Extras								$3.00	$4.50	$1.25	$10.25
Leaving anything out (toys, movies, games, etc.)	Each Occurance	All	($0.50)					$0.00	$0.00	$0.00	$0.00
Leaving trash out	Each Occurance	All	($0.50)					$0.00	$0.00	$0.00	$0.00
								$45.50	$33.00	$17.25	$48.25

Figure 3: Screen Shot of Chore Worksheet

Figure 4: Our Chore Corner

Notes:

Use the following pages for your reflections. These reflections will help you decide how to maximize the chore system for your unique family.

Challenge 1: Everyone can afford it

Write down everything, and I mean everything, that you have gotten extra for your family this month.

_____
_____
_____
_____
_____
_____
_____
_____
_____
_____
_____
_____
_____
_____
_____
_____
_____
_____
_____
_____
_____
_____
_____
_____
_____
_____
_____
_____
_____
_____
_____
_____
_____

Challenge 2: Less stress

Make a list of all your stresses. If possible, have your kids do the same. This is a private exercise you can decide to share with each other or not.

_____
_____
_____
_____
_____
_____
_____
_____
_____
_____
_____
_____
_____
_____
_____
_____
_____
_____
_____
_____
_____
_____
_____
_____
_____
_____
_____
_____
_____
_____
_____
_____

Challenge 3: Chores to be set by age and ability

Think about what your children would like to do to help you. Ask them.

_____
_____
_____
_____
_____
_____
_____
_____
_____
_____
_____
_____
_____
_____
_____
_____
_____
_____
_____
_____
_____
_____
_____
_____
_____
_____
_____
_____
_____
_____
_____
_____
_____
_____
_____

Challenge 4: Experts and paying for chores

What do you think about paying your children for chores? Should they be paid for everything or just certain chores?

_____
_____
_____
_____
_____
_____
_____
_____
_____
_____
_____
_____
_____
_____
_____
_____
_____
_____
_____
_____
_____
_____
_____
_____
_____
_____
_____
_____
_____
_____
_____
_____
_____

Challenge 5: When is the proper age to start?

Write down a description of your kids. What do you think their challenges will be, and what will be your solutions?

Challenge 6: Dream and dream big.

Write down all your goals. Be outrageous. No one else has to see them. This is just for you. If possible, have your kids do this too.

_____
_____
_____
_____
_____
_____
_____
_____
_____
_____
_____
_____
_____
_____
_____
_____
_____
_____
_____
_____
_____
_____
_____
_____
_____
_____
_____
_____
_____
_____
_____
_____
_____
_____
_____

Challenge 7: "I spent all my money. Can I have $20 for . . . ?"

Get out that pencil; try to think of all the extras the kids may hit you up for. Write down creative ways of saying no.

_____

_____

_____

_____

_____

_____

_____

_____

_____

_____

_____

_____

_____

_____

_____

_____

_____

_____

_____

_____

_____

_____

_____

_____

_____

_____

_____

_____

_____

_____

_____

_____

_____

_____

_____

_____

The Solution: The Chore System

Look over your notes and see how simple this chore system will work for you! This is the time for you to add or subtract your ideas to make this chore system work for you.

Reference List

Aquirre, S. Age appropriate chore charts. *About.com: Housekeeping*, http://housekeeping.about.com/od/chorechart1/a/ageapprchores.htm (retrieved July 11, 2010).

Bay, W. 2010. Buffett recounts the best advice he's ever received. Yahoo News: http://www.someaddress.com/full/url/

(retrieved July 8, 2010).

Cline, M. F., J. Stern, and B. Zucker. 2010. Chores vs. allowance: To pay or not to pay (January 7). *ParentsAsk.com*, http://www.parentsask.com/preteen/allowance/chores-vs-allowance-pay-or-not-pay-video.html (retrieved July 8, 2010).

Goodwill. http://www.goodwill.org/ (retrieved July 15, 2010).

Kirsch, M. 2008. Should parents pay kids for chores? *The Times* (March 8), http://women.timesonline.co.uk/tol/life_and_style/women/body_and_soul/article3503680.ece (retrieved July 8, 2010).

The Salvation Army. http://www.salvationarmyusa.org/usn/www_usn_2.nsf/vw-local/Home (retrieved July 15, 2010).